Passageways

OTHER BOOKS BY
PHILIP RESNICK

POETRY

Poems for Andromache (1975)

Poems of Pelion (1979)

The Centaur's Mountain (1986)

Footsteps of the Past (2015)

NON-FICTION

The Land of Cain (1977)

Parliament vs. People (1984)

Letters to a Québécois Friend (1990)

The Masks of Proteus: Canadian Reflections on the State (1990)

Toward a Canada-Quebec Union (1991)

Thinking English Canada (1994)

Twenty-First Century Democracy (1997)

The Politics of Resentment: British Columbia Regionalism and Canadian Unity (2000)

The European Roots of Canadian Identity (2005)

The Labyrinth of North American Identities (2012)

Passageways

PHILIP RESNICK

RONSDALE

RONSDALE PRESS
3350 West 21st Avenue, Vancouver, B.C., Canada V6S 1G7
www.ronsdalepress.com

Typesetting: Julie Cochrane, in New Baskerville 11 pt on 13.5
Cover Design: Julie Cochrane
Paper: Enviro 100 Edition, 55 lb. Antique Cream (FSC®) — 100% post-consumer waste, totally chlorine-free and acid-free

Ronsdale Press wishes to thank the following for their support of its publishing program: the Canada Council for the Arts, the Government of Canada through the Canada Book Fund, the British Columbia Arts Council, and the Province of British Columbia through the Book Publishing Tax Credit Program.

Library and Archives Canada Cataloguing in Publication

Resnick, Philip, 1944–, author
  Passageways / Philip Resnick. — First edition.

Poems.
Issued in print and electronic formats.
ISBN 978-1-55380-523-6 (softcover)
ISBN 978-1-55380-524-3 (ebook) / ISBN 978-1-55380-525-0 (pdf)

  I. Title.

PS8585.E8P37 2018   C811'.54   C2018-900528-9   C2018-900529-7

At Ronsdale Press we are committed to protecting the environment. To this end we are working with Canopy and printers to phase out our use of paper produced from ancient forests. This book is one step towards that goal.

Printed in Canada by Marquis Book Printing, Quebec, Canada

in memory of A.V.R.,
much loved, much missed

ACKNOWLEDGEMENTS

I wish to extend my thanks to Jonah Resnick whose photos of a passageway through the olive grove in Damouchari at the base of Mount Pelion inspired the idea for the cover, and to Julie Cochrane for the cover design, also to Ronald Hatch for his helpful editorial suggestions, and to the public policy journal *Inroads*, where a number of the political poems first appeared.

TO THE READER

There is a wide range of themes in this collection, reflecting writing that in some cases goes back over forty years. The first section contains a selection of poems many of which appeared in books first published in the 1970s or 1980s and long since out of print, *Poems for Andromache, Poems of Pelion,* and *The Centaur's Mountain.*

The poems in the second section touch on places to which I have had occasion to travel, sometimes for conferences or pursuant to academic activities, e.g. Spain, France, Argentina, Japan, and Central Europe, or in the case of Greece, my late wife's homeland and very much a second home for our family over many years.

The third section, not surprisingly for someone who for over four decades taught political science at the University of British Columbia, touches on political themes. Most of these poems are of recent vintage, commenting on developments both international and Canadian, sometimes as a direct reaction to events of the day, sometimes in a more muted and indirect way.

The fourth section contains reflections, often inspired by passages and books from a range of poets and writers; sundry thoughts which have come to me as the years run along, and the occasional autobiographical poem.

The poems in the last section were the most difficult for me to write, for it is here that I deal with the death of a loved one. This was my unhappy experience in 2016, as my wife was dying. The poems reflect my attempts to deal with the greatest challenge we all have to face.

Philip Resnick
Vancouver, Spring 2018

CONTENTS

– IV –
MEDITATIONS AND
REFLECTIONS

– V –

THANATOS'S
SHADOW

Passageways

You came to grieve
on Pelion
home of Chiron
the healing centaur.
You came to renew bonds
with the mountain's vegetation,
its soaring cliffs,
its temperamental sea.
You came to hear the voice
that through the years
inspired your verse.
Lastly you came looking
for passageways ahead
through dark terrain and olive groves
deceptively uncharted.

OF THE GREEKS
AND HEBREWS

Jason

"O my country: What fond memories
I have of thee at this hour."
— Euripides, *Medea*

Once eating from her lips and skin
swearing by Zeus and the Olympians
vows to last forever.
Then hungering after richer fare
cold hellos, goodbyes, icy kisses.
Till in the heat of early afternoon,
cicadas worked into a frenzy,
he comes with news of fresh elopement.
There is no hope for what is dead,
no resurrecting father, brothers, homeland overseas.
Still, those who live will learn
what pains a lover takes with traitors.
First princess, indifferent to *her* sorrow,
will burn in robes of fire,
then children,
like unripe figs plucked from their mother's breast,
will curse blade hurtling them to Hades,
while he, two-bit philanderer,
will end his days drifting from *taverna* to *taverna*,
spurned by the better whores,
scabrous at the foreskin.

Phaedra

"Aphrodite! Now I see that she is not a mere
god but some force far mightier than that."
— Euripides, *Hippolytus*

She seeks him at night,
reaching hand across pillow,
brushing fireplace with fingertips.
The young man turns his flank,
smiles in his sleep, a scar on his left cheek
marks scenes of bitter argument last week
with his stepmother.
Over the house,
perfume of gardenias freshly blooming,
in the courtyard almond trees and lemons.
An unlit corridor separates the sweating woman
from her wish.

Iphigenia

Snow is falling over Montparnasse
as we leave the cinema,
sacrificial smoke still circling altar,
unseen blade.
Clytemnestra's eyes rage at the sailing fleet,
rehearsing vengeance for spouse's bloodied crown.
In this rendition no afterlife
no rendezvous at Tauris
where mad Orestes, fleeing his mother's furies,
can find solace in his sister's arms.
Alone she walks towards death
as she has done ten thousand times since that fateful year
when Spartan armies bearing down on Athens
gave playwright theme.
And if Cacoyannis takes liberties with the text
does it much matter
which of the gods or spiteful Calchas does her in?
Her corpse is but a testament
to that fine line separating barbarian from Greek,
civilization from its reptilian brain,
melting in the brazen heat of vanished Aulis.

Astyanax

*"Now Andromache ran to her bronze-clad
husband, and the nurse was with her,
holding a little boy in her arms, a baby son,
Hector's bright star, Astyanax."*
—— *Iliad*, Book VI

Through battles thick she shielded him
far from swirling dust of plain
until the morning (he was still a babe)
she held him next to ramparts,
watching his father slain by Chiron's charge, Peleus's son.
What happened next is none too clear,
some say his widowed mother torn by grief
sought vengeance on the Spartan whore,
others that days were spent
between shrine and darkened home,
pouring libations for her cremated spouse.
When the hour came that Themis had foretold
he clung to apron strings hoping against hope
for reprieve from the blade.
Still five, he found each moment lengthening
as a youth, then man, then elder of his city
he won great glory for his father's name
and heard his mother's virtues sung.
Seized at last by savage hands he bared his breast,
showing how even children shortchange death.

Of the Ancients

Why do their legends seem embedded in our memes,
as though we were condemned to repeat
the hubris, the untamed erotic lust,
the wiliness, the misplaced trust
that so often spelled disaster?
The polis is no more,
the smoking altars,
the oracles with their cryptic pronouncements,
the Olympian Pantheon, the blind prophet.
Yet one plunges and re-plunges into a familiar matrix,
and listening to the Aegean
rolling in at evening on a tiny Pelion cove,
it is as though a Sophoclean chorus
were warning of approaching storms.

Narcissus

Fleeing men and women
city, fields and home
he came to a forest clearing
where rippling waters run,
a shape elusive calling to him from the edge,
"Come, come . . ."
His pride, so difficult, so stubborn,
melted at its sight,
a power greater than his own
reached out for pining lips
pulling downwards, ever downwards
to where a god-like figure sleeps.

Ariadne's Thread

Through the labyrinth he moves
in dust-covered sandals,
searching for the stalking one,
and when at the foreshadowed hour he strikes
and the bull-headed monster,
our half-brother,
has been dispatched,
one part of his labour is accomplished.
He must now retrace his steps
past twisted corridors that resemble one another
and mirror each other's faults.
Only then does he remember Ariadne's thread,
her life-giving thread
that will lead back into the known world.
But as for Ariadne,
her love will languish unrequited
on the long journey back,
abandoned, threadless
in mid-Aegean.

Sappho

Sea reflected light from spume of waves,
clouds bespoke poems springing from island's stones,
yet streets slept undisturbed.
True that night at the festival
a young woman led her troupe in costumed dance,
eyes blazing, girdles tightly bound,
cobbled square echoing to re-enactment of Hymen's bond.
The islanders had heard such oaths a hundred times,
none noticed the intensity of hands clasped to breasts,
stroking thighs, miming the very act of love.
None but she who, stealthily with a kiss,
had taught her sisters what the gods had missed.

Of the Muses

Of the muses
Clio has been the most persistent
with your penchant for people's uprisings
shifting credos,
and the grand movements of imperia and armies.
Next has been Erato,
short bursts of verse to colour a grey landscape
and give fitful expression to emotions
that might otherwise lurk forever in the background.
Euterpe, Thalia, Terpsichore, Urania
have never been your stalwarts,
Calliope beyond your reach,
with Polyhymnia the occasional companion
to your poetic capers.
As old age seeps in,
more and more you dwell in the shadow of Melpomene,
stern in her bearing,
weighed down by the sheer perversity
of an intractable human condition.

Melpomene: the Greek muse of tragedy.

The Greek Alphabet

You cannot share a love
for the Greek church or for its rituals,
its incense, icons, candles,
you who have firmly turned your back
on all religions.
But the Greek alphabet has a charm
that quite beguiles you,
double consonants like xs,
ps, th, and ph,
the lovely patterns the letters make
printed upon the page,
even as passages from the ancients
reverberate in your head
and poems from the moderns spin their web.

Matters of Faith

"Very few Greeks are devout."
— Aliki Bacopoulouhalls, *Modern Greek Theatre*

You wonder as you watch older passengers on the bus
cross themselves three times
whenever they pass a village cemetery or church.
You wonder when every lurching, winding road
boasts a tiny chapel to those who perished at the wheel.
You wonder when saint days are still the norm,
church memorials for the dead after 40 days,
pilgrimages to shrines like Tinos
with their waxen limbs on sale.
Faith has a way
of worming itself into the soul
and refusing to let go.

Joseph

In Genesis, recognition comes in the final pages,
in *Iphigenia in Tauris* towards the middle.
Either way the theme of a long-lost sibling
coming back from the dead
grips both monotheists and pagans.
Is it because we ourselves have doubts
how far our love for a parent's offspring carries,
or that millennia of civil strife
make the weight of kinsmen's betrayal
stain more than rainbow coats?
Those who meet again after untold tribulations
have learned what desert wastes separate
a Joseph from his brothers.

Moses

Of the hundred questions I'd have asked you
back then when I was still a boy,
only one remains —
what made you so certain of your mission,
giving you courage to match wits against the Pharaoh?
I know what religious lore will answer,
burning bush, Jehovah, the suffering of Jacob's children,
but between us, Moses, was there no other motivation?
I half suspect in the dry desert heat
white robes, grey hair flowing,
yours was a tantalizing vision —
leading Israel out of exile towards the promised land
and on the way achieving what only a bare handful
have since attempted: a new religion,
lawgiver and potentate combined.
Is this the Moses that my ancestors followed,
the man of power,
who once in a people's lifetime,
sets its world on fire?

Samson

Blinding sun played tricks with memory,
melting jaw bones into clubs,
asses into gold-maned lions
roaming desert sands.
His tresses newly growing
crowned a head that once had nestled
in Delilah's folds.
Rings of Philistines made light
of the padlocked champion of the Israelites
leading him like a beast of burden
to where Dagan's temple arrogantly rose.
Sweat dotting forehead, torso, limbs,
he grasped two pillars between his failing hands,
but as he bent a thousand muscles strained
and a hidden god surged through his ligaments.

Jonathan

Had he been Greek,
the story might have ended more predictably,
a soldier dying in his comrade's arms,
a helot side by side with nobleman.
His was a harsher race,
no goat- or horse-like creatures
frolicking in Samaria's wastes.
A prince of the Hebrews,
he hid his feelings amidst parables and furtive looks,
rendezvousing in fields far from the capital,
where brimstone showered down on sodomites.
His father's curse made David yet more comely in his eyes,
golden tresses set against a shepherd's garb,
a stripling still, when slaying mastodon,
his sling had won great glory for the king.
Embracing on the eve of battle
which Ein Dor's witch foretold
spelled certain death,
Jonathan wept,
but David, kissing him a final time,
saw the road opening to the throne.

Ezekiel

"The hand of the Lord was upon me,
and set me down in the midst of a valley,
which was full of bones."

— *Ezekiel,* 37:1

Neither as chiliastic as the first Isaiah
nor as lugubrious as Jeremiah,
his was a more balanced prophetic vision.
A touch of anger,
appropriate to one of his vocation,
mingled with a healing hand.
Who else visiting the vale of death
would have felt the breath of times to come
able to infuse new life into the dry bones
all tribes and peoples are destined to rejoin?
No false solution his,
promising individual resurrection,
but paleontology almost scientific,
making of skulls and cartilage
the future's building stones.

In Alexandria

In Alexandria
you might have had to choose
between the austere religion
of the Abrahamic god,
its desert cult,
its 613 laws so strict
they drove its acolytes to self-abnegation,
and the subtle logic of the Hellenistic schools
embedded in a polytheistic frame,
reflecting the four elements,
a geometric and cosmic turn,
accompanied by the sensuous beauty of the flesh
on parade in the gymnasium
and the market.
You know from your heart
which you would have chosen,
an apostate to the synagogue
and its commandments,
to the seclusion the offspring of Jacob cherished,
opting instead for companions
among the Alexandrians.
For you were not born to be faithful
to precepts of a rigid code,
yet even in betrayal
would have remained loyal
to the old faith's prophetic undercurrent.

The God that Failed

The Jews, writes Jonathan Sacks,
with their faith in the Eternal,
had little place for the Greek version of the tragic.
But the tragic had a way of forcing itself
through crevices the Eternal had left uncovered
into the interstices of their historical narrative,
leaving Oedipus, Cassandra, and Electra
gasping from the sidelines.

Jonathan Sacks: Emeritus Chief Rabbi of the Commonwealth and author of
To Heal a Fractured World.

Diáspora Sefardí

Translucent as ever her voice,
evoking far-flung corners of the diaspora that fled
in the aftermath of the Catholic monarchs' blood decrees.
Montserrat Figueras herself is no more,
and what you hear are imprints of a tongue,
which survives her disappearance.
Catalans, who bore their own cross for centuries,
can well understand the pain that filters through these songs,
tempered by viola, flute and harp.
She brings again to life laments and tears,
fantasies and dreams,
offshoots of an exiled land.

Montserrat Figueras: the lead singer on music recorded by Hespèrion XXI,
with Jordi Savall the director of this Catalan-based ensemble.

Jerusalem

Jerusalem has been redeemed,
millennial promises fulfilled,
cries that reached the heavens
and fell again like broken shards to earth,
no longer plaintive orphans
in a land that gave them birth.
Jerusalem has been redeemed
and all seems as luminous as can be
to those who follow every letter of the law,
walking in footpaths that the ancient texts prescribe.
Jerusalem has been redeemed
amidst tawny stones and golden dome,
yet half the city mourns its shattered dreams
as old tales of victimhood and new begin to merge.

Jewish Intellectuals

A touchy subject really
as enough blood has drenched Europe's soil and rivers
without my reviving atavistic hate
for people of my childhood faith.

But the pages of literary journals,
scientific discourse, musical disputation
and other branches of *Weltwissenschaft*
were for so long the lungs and air
of these amphibious creatures
— neither of the gentile world, nor of their own —
it forces me to ponder.

Even today, when in liberal democratic states
most feel quite rooted,
there's far more than a sprinkling of our stock
in areas of intellectual endeavour.

Can it be genetics?
I am not certain what the latest findings would divulge,
but I shudder at the thought
that somewhere in our chromosomes
little Einsteins, bearded Freuds,
chutzpah-driven novelists
and haunted ones like Kafka or like Zweig
tussle to see the light.

Can it be folk culture,
music, always minor, always whining,
a bookishness transmitted from the Talmud?
Perhaps, but culture in this century has broadened,
and amidst the literate masses,
who from the Orient and Old World to the New
form legion upon legion,
can Jews assume they still have special status?

Maybe things are simpler —
the Jews having learned from Ricardo and from Marx
about comparative advantage and commodity exchange
branched out into neglected sectors.
Why not the avant-garde and therapists,
muckrakers and moralists,
dishevelled scientists and iconoclastic seekers
of the Western world?

– II –

FARAWAY
SHORES

Unstrung Guitar

The crossroads as you travelled from Cádiz
pointed north or east,
one fork towards Cordova and Sevilla
with their vaunted treasure troves,
the other towards Grenada with its Moorish palisade.
The heart said "Go eastwards,"
aïe, aïe, aïe,
as a Gitan's cry
pierced bleeding landscape and moonless sky.
But the head longed for other destinations,
pillared mosques, glittering cathedrals,
Sephardic traces, archives of the unfathomable Indies.

Habitación 228, Residencia de Estudiantes, Madrid

You return to the silence of your *Residencia* room,
but you are not alone.
You hear the ineffable sounds
of conversations past and interlocutors vanished.
You write with a confidence
that comes from tapping sibylline places,
walled-up chambers opening to the invitation
to share their inner spaces.

The Residencia de Estudiantes, founded in the early 20th century as a
student residence in Madrid with such future alumni as Lorca, Dali, and
Buñuel, is now a facility for cultural activities and visiting faculty.

Passeig de Gràcia

You come looking for traces of your eighteen years.
The pattern of side streets vaguely seems the same,
buildings where the principal avenues intersect.
The rest is blank,
like the office where you worked that summer of '63,
the rented room on the nearby Calle del Bruc,
the smart shops quite unlike the sleepy storefronts
when El caudillo held this city in his sway.
Most of all it is the eighteen years you'll never find again.

El caudillo: the name by which Francisco Franco was known, just as Mussolini
was known as Il duce.

Praza das Praterías,
Santiago de Compostela

They wait in various states of expectancy
for the Corpus Christi procession to begin,
a velvet altar in the square
festooned with lilies and a golden spire.
The band lines up
as does an honour guard in medieval uniform,
two boys with candles lit,
priests in full regalia,
white-robed novices with crosses in their hand.
Bells ring out,
a joyous sound for those
who wend their way through Santiago's narrow streets.
So must a crowd have gathered to watch
five centuries ago
the lighting of the Holy Inquisition's fires.

Metropolitan Museum

Already they begin to fade,
whirl of Manets, Monets,
Byzantine or Cypriot art,
Islamic ceramics, Japanese floral arrangements,
as late afternoon descends on the city
and Sunday crowds disperse to their sundry vocations.
You sit in the nearby park
ruminating on your hurried visit
to the museum, to the Upper West Side,
and on a family bar mitzvah
that cannot revive a long-lapsed faith.

Kyoto Passage

The sun illuminates the hills
that ring this temple town
and soon its early morning hues
will turn to lighter shades,
blending into the rooftops and the trees.
Kanji shapes dance in your head,
Hiragana characters form and reform
like double-braided chromosomes.
Your lectures draw to a close,
already you must say your last farewells,
Kiyomizu's pillars and Nijo-jo's massive wooden doors
stare you down.

Quarter Moon

Stationed in the night sky
it stands vigil over a sleeping city,
with the observer too awake to sleep.
Tomorrow is today,
you leave for home in the morning,
and come home in the morning of the same day.
Kyoto moon,
keep me company,
bridge the gap.

In Borges's City

Did Borges come to this square,
across from the Museo,
by the fashion-conscious Alvear?
Do motorized sounds,
mixing with acoustical guitars,
evoke some passage in "The Aleph,"
or the enigmatic moment when god suspended time
to let a playwright complete his masterwork?
This city has a soul
and its chroniclers have found
amidst labyrinths that twist and turn,
European shadows,
libraries of imaginary worlds,
the muse's calling.

Cementerio de la Recoleta, 1991

Past chiselled tombs,
crypts of publishers, cardiologists and rectors
ministering to the soul or body,
along the alleyways of a deserted city,
no blade of grass to disturb the grey cement and marble,
you wander.
A cat or two has made a home
amongst these necro-villas with their coffins,
while guardians tend to the flowers and the dust,
sweeping the portals clean,
much as concierges might do in the world of the living.
Suddenly around the bend TV cameras whir,
a whole cortège of mourners
— wreaths of the finest roses, orchids at their feet —
has gathered around the Duarte tomb
to mark the 39th year since her passing.
A balding trumpeter, out of a '30s movie,
plays in her honour, as a sea of hands,
each with two fingers held aloft, salutes to the cry
"Viva Perón!" "Viva Eva Perón!" "Viva la patria!"
Many of the women are in furs,
a few in simpler cloth or woolens,
their eyes moistening to the power of a legend.
Which is the real Evita,
the stricken saint they mourn,
Madonna to the impoverished *Descamisados*,
heroine of Broadway musicals?
Or the spider lady behind a fickle demagogue
who for decades kept a country in his thrall?

María Eva Duarte de Perón (7 May 1919–26 July 1952) was the wife
of Juan Perón. She is buried in the Cementerio de la Recoleta.

In a Provençal Town, circa 1220 AD

Paratge has long since fled the city gates
and sulfurous smells rising from the pyres
where Cathars burn
would stain the heavens yellow
while a cloud of flies
insufferable in the summer heat
swarms overhead.
Why have so many died,
why does hatred replace courtly love with lies,
dogma laced with empty rites,
the friars' cruel intolerance?
The world has little place
for the simple and the pure
and songs that spell romance
will nevermore be heard.

Paratge: the Provençal term for right living, civility, grace and nobility of soul.

Cité Universitaire

That faraway spring
that brought the two of us together
at the Maison des Étudiants Canadiens,
after we had travelled to the Loire
in a growing infatuation,
craving each other's presence,
the voice, the sensuous touch,
the limbs which Eros seemed to have fashioned.
Today this all comes back to you,
as though she were alive.

Maison de Culture, Bobigny

It's overcast when they put on the Hölderlin play
at the Maison de Culture on the boulevard Lénine
as children from western Africa and the Maghreb
play soccer beneath the high-rise towers.
One enters into a literary darkness
in the nearer Parisian suburbs this Sunday afternoon,
and the ever-receding ancients
rock us in their arms.

Trade Fair Palace, Prague, 1942

They had been herded together in the early hours,
a hard snow falling on the muffled streets,
their warm clothes, silverware, jewellery,
heaped in piles
as they waited, days on end,
for transport to some fabled sanctuary,
a Terezin where art and music
would momentarily dissolve the hunger and cold
wracking their bones,
even as the cruel beating of the guards,
the public hangings,
mocked prospects of any human embrace.

Olympus

In the shadow of Olympus,
snow-capped and multi-peaked
as the epic poet once described it,
water coursing from its summit,
beech and white pine canopying its slopes,
we descend steep stony trails,
a pool with tadpoles at one turn,
wooden bridges, alpine flowers,
and suddenly a burst of thunder,
as though the gods,
invisible and immortal,
would make their presence known.
We take shelter beside an old monastery
with the pagan-sounding name Saint Dionysius,
that like an interloper
inserts itself where the Olympians once dwelt.
And then, as though in resolution
of the lingering religious conflict,
a rainbow with its arch of colours,
and a hint of sunshine over the town of Litochoro
and the Aegean far below.

Kiki's House

The old house lies in ruins,
its pink walls exposed,
an abortive staircase pointing up
to what was once a fabled second storey.
Nature reclaims the grounds,
ivy, thorns, and ferns
free at last to propagate,
while fig tree stumps stand guard
like refugees from a forgotten war.
The grounds retain a measure of serenity
looking towards the sea,
and for a moment one catches glimpses
of vanished majesty and power.

Flowers of Pelion

One could make a botanical dispensary
out of what Pelion has to offer,
valerian and oleander,
spearmint and euphorbia,
yarrow and St. John's wort,
set amidst the silver limes and yews,
oriental planes and common aspen,
black alders and Judas trees
that dot the mountain's landscape.
Just gazing at the colours of its flowers,
or relishing the mellowness
with which the sun beams down
in the early hours
or watching currents in the water
set against its darkened foliage
can make one grateful
for Pelion's healing touch.

The Gentleman Caller

Like a figure out of a Cavafy poem
he came down the winding path to the village house
in his Panama hat, formal tie and jacket,
to offer greetings to the household's aging matron.
His demeanour was extremely polite,
and his posture, though slightly stooped,
of someone who had known glorious days
in the Egyptian cotton trade between the wars.
You shook his hand,
both when he came and parted,
but it felt as though an apparition
had graced the doorway.

Olive Trees

*"Never conquered,
a terror to our enemies and their spears,
the grey-leafed olive."*
— Sophocles, *Oedipus at Colonus*

When the old master
spoke of olive trees
as the mountain's terror
it seemed a lofty parable.
But here, in the full-day sun,
the brightness of their silvery leaves
blinds you like the flash of swords
amidst boulders and red clay.

The Muse

Within the Damouchari house's thick stone walls
your muse must have been hiding,
waiting for the scribbler from afar,
ministering to an ailing spouse,
to journey back again.
Muses too grow lonely
despite the beauty Pelion has to offer,
and the interrupted dialogue you've had with one another,
made painful by the many years you could not be together,
can finally resume.

Damouchari: a small cove on the east coast of Pelion.

Daybreak over Damouchari

A medley of pastel shades
through the latticed window
as daybreak over the horizon
inaugurates another cycle.
For the ancients,
a source of wonder,
stirring the imagination
to feats of creativity and innovation.
For apocalyptical seers,
proof of a divinity beyond the clouds,
shaping the mysteries of a finite world
and sinful mortals dwelling therein.
As for us moderns,
jaded in our comforts,
secular in temper,
rational in our judgments,
a wake-up call at 6 AM
to a sense of awe we have forgotten.

Thalassa

The waters roll in on Pelion's shores
as they've rolled for thousands of years
and the stories they'd tell
were they able to speak,
might resemble the ones
which sailors devised
as they skirted its coves and its cliffs.
The voice of the sea
is a different voice from our own
and the sights it has seen
and the ships it conveyed
and the deaths it has borne
are lost in the spume of its waves.

Thalassa: the Greek word for sea.

The Surf

Record the sound of the surf
rolling in from Halkidiki.
Play it back at night
when you are insomniac.
Close your eyes,
letting your body gently sway
and your muscles relax,
as the force of the waves overwhelms
saudade that pulls towards the dark.

Saudade: a feeling of longing, melancholy, or nostalgia that is supposedly
characteristic of the Portuguese or Brazilian temperament.

Homage to Chiron

When I came here in the autumn
it was already too cold
to sit out in the evening hours
listening to chestnuts hit the ground.
My notebook was largely blank
and my psyche was seeking
a healer's balm.
Growing accustomed to the natural cycle,
to waking by myself with the first rays over the Aegean
and forcing my lazy hand to scribble
I became emboldened with fall's colours.
Then came the winter,
and leaving this house I revered above all others,
I sought your presence in the city below,
and even further, in distant lands and across waters,
where centaurs never ventured.
Till returning in the spring,
I sit intoxicated by the warbling of nightingales and wrens,
and the dark foliage that clothes your mountain.
Can I be so ungrateful, Chiron,
not to offer you these lines?

The Voice

Soon the god's voice will be stilled,
and this scene
— red sun in a perfect ball over the Aegean —
will be consigned to the blue squares of your writing book,
no more alive than a butterfly or leaf between two sheets.
The lapping on this cove
that rocks you gently in your sleep
and greets you at first break
you'll try to summon up where evenings are cold
and sunlight is steadily in retreat
— to no avail.
For this god's mark is never to be felt a second time,
not when you venture far from Pelion's peaks
and shelters where he resides.
What you have seen and heard
was not for you to will —
from this week forth the voice grows still.

– III –

IN TROUBLED
TIMES

Winterschlaf

We have entered the season of hibernation,
the damp cold months
when all hope of radical transformation
gives way to the subterranean powers of eternal yesterday,
the aristocracy of wealth,
the hierarchs of unchecked authority,
the preachers of apocalyptical creeds.
One waits in vain to hear
from the watchman on the tower,
that over the horizon daylight breaks.
For the moment sleep pervades.

Heinrich Heine referred to the period 1815–1848, when progressive
politics in Europe was repressed in the aftermath of the Congress of
Vienna, as *Winterschlaf*.

Paradise Lost

On Utoeya Island, no Utopia now,
adolescent bodies lie scattered,
as merciless rounds
gun a political generation down.
No quarter from a gunman
with his cultivated Facebook pose
and rabid determination
to turn an open welfare state around.
A near-perfect score on the Human Development Index
can provide little relief from dark recesses
that surge out of the Viking past,
passion trumping reason every odd day of the week.

Utoeya is the Norwegian island on which Anders Behring Breivik
murdered 69 people, in addition to the eight he had killed previously
in an Oslo bombing.

Le défi

The future is beyond our horizon
and the past retreats at a frightening speed.
Most in the developed West do not live in dark times,
but beyond the epidermis of our planet darkness reigns,
and looming within the hearts of our fellow humans
it always threatens.
Amidst the patter of unfamiliar tongues,
global disruptions, and nativist rebellion,
an atavistic current surges.

Alexanderplatz

Old Believers inured in their faith
in a Party and a cause that never can do wrong,
Babushkas with memories of the Steppes,
Muttis whose wild flings amidst the cacti and the Aztec ruins
haunt them until their dying days,
those who come of age oblivious to the lies their elders told,
and a regime that lived its forty years
amidst the ruins of a still more hateful one,
snow blowing through Alexanderplatz,
Trabants puttering, district secretaries muttering,
discordant, shattered lives.

This poem was inspired by my reading of Eugen Ruge's *In Times of Fading Light*, a novel touching on three generations who lived in the former G.D.R./East Germany.

Fugue

for Liu Xiaobo, in memoriam

How still the night
and plangent the sound of distant sobbing,
for death doesn't pause
even for a moment
and the tales poets tell
as they weave their epic lines
about battles lost and won,
sacrifices for noble causes,
love that doesn't falter in the breach,
are soon dissolved,
as the vow to speak one's mind
seals one's fate.

Liu Xiaobo was the dissident Chinese intellectual and poet who kept vigil at
Tiananmen Square in 1989 to protect protesters from encroaching soldiers
and who promoted a pro-democracy charter that brought him a lengthy
prison sentence. He was awarded the Nobel Peace Prize and died under
guard in hospital.

The Better Angels of Our Nature

Deaths keep adding up,
in sunflower fields in the Donetsk,
Baghdad on a market day,
Aleppo, Gaza, South Sudan,
Northern Nigeria where Boko Haram reigns.
True, mass armies don't line up
as in world wars,
and great powers,
though they play their cloak-and-dagger games,
resist the atavistic urge to go for each other's vital parts.
But as a new century hobbles along,
only cave dwellers could greet the vultures overhead
as birds of song.

Sans Illusions

Soon enough broken promises come home
and we are left to pay the debt —
5,000 years of debt —
that others issued in our name.
If we dare raise our voices in disdain,
for a system that has come unstuck,
there are ground troops and information warriors
to put us down.
For wealth has little place for sentiment
and treats dissent with a contempt
that those with power effortlessly reinvent.
Somewhere in the second balcony
someone whispers the word "democracy,"
to no avail;
for it too has accumulated a crushing debt
of promises only rarely kept.

The Paradise Papers

"Not Caesar now, but money, is all."
—Alain de Lille, 12th-century monk

So the Fourth Estate has come to our rescue,
telling truths about power
that the powerful only whisper to themselves.
Will it change an iota
now that we know the feints and subterfuges
by which fortunes can escape
the gatekeepers meant to keep
the ship of state afloat —
where rock stars rub shoulders with royals,
political fundraisers with CEOs,
in the game of tax evasion and high finance?
Age-old suspicions will be confirmed,
a few indignant voices will be stirred,
as the masters of the universe carry on undeterred
in worshiping the deity that reigns on earth.

Deontology

The morning news with its toll of deaths
— be it London, Kabul or godforsaken Yemen —
is as grim as ever
and it seems almost obscene,
as the Rohingyas flee Myanmar
and refugee camps overfill their quotas,
to be sheltered in an idyllic Pelion cove
watching morning waves over the Aegean.
But did the world stop
for Auschwitz or Hiroshima,
and can we ever right the balance
between those whose lives
will run a normal course
and those who'll live theirs
in mutilated fractions?

Deontology: rule-based ethics.

Getting to Denmark

At one level,
all you need to do is purchase the fare,
find an accommodating B&B
somewhere in the outskirts of Aarhus or Copenhagen
and enjoy the scene.
Smorrebrod and decent beer,
clean energy and lots of country air,
a government that works
and social policies the envy of the globe.

At another level,
we never will get there,
for even little Denmark
can never attain a perfect score.
Its migrants don't quite belong,
its Rimbauds have been known to overdose,
its bankers and merchant fleet
are as rapacious as the *Argo*'s sailors
seeking the Golden Fleece.

Francis Fukuyama in his book *Political Order and Political Decay* (2014) has a
chapter holding up Denmark as the model to which states should aspire.

Political Cycles

Great hopes become great lies
as mantras that held one-third of humanity in thrall
succumb to the new flavour of the age,
Market-Leninism giving a gentle shove
to the previous Marxist-Leninist credo that sought,
with passion and with blood,
to storm the heavens,
whatever the means, whatever the cost.

In the Balkans

In the Balkans,
where recognition was a perennial battle
and nationalism drew first blood,
the previous century was born.
For the springtime of the peoples
proved a graveyard for the losers
and a trial run for the thick carapace
linking language, ethnicity, state
— and why fool ourselves? — religion
through much of our divided planet.
The unwieldy empires of old,
with their sultans, kaisers, and emperors,
have lost their sway
but we, who follow in their aftermath,
are stumbling as we seek our way.

Inspired by my reading the *Report of the International Commission to Inquire into the Causes and Conduct of the Balkan Wars*, 1914, with its account of atrocities committed by all sides to the conflict.

Yin and Yang

In the north
citizens pay their taxes, at least mostly,
institutions generally function
and promises that political leaders make
are usually kept — although sometimes broken.
Most are driven by self-interest,
but do not neglect the commons
in their more reflective moments,
although interpersonal relations are measured
and passions confined to favourite sporting teams
and such like matters.

In the south,
where flouting fiscal obligations is legion
along with treating the public realm
as something of a wishing well,
a different ethos is in order.
There is warmth to human interactions,
a deeper sense of familial obligations,
a greater proximity to life's mysteries and cycles,
as though the sun at its noon-day zenith
had seared itself into the psyche.

Europa after the Rain

In its own inimitable way,
Europe undoes the stitches that bind its wounds,
north against south,
the frugal ones against the party-goers,
disenchantment seeping through the corridors
where emissaries meet for negotiations without end,
Penelope's thread unable to withstand
the constant fraying, the weather-beaten elements,
for the continent has too many mountain ranges,
verdant islands, rivers coursing through its veins
to be a single integrated space,
and already the ghosts of Holy Roman Empires past,
Napoleonic conceits, and Congresses to spell an end to war
remind the chastened eavesdropper at the door
that dreams and nightmares are really twins
and fir trees and olive groves
silent witnesses to all that came before.

In Postmodern Times

Old forms dissolve
as the fragments are rearranged
in a smorgasbord of asymmetrical shapes
with labels like discourse theory,
liquid reality, risk society.
Yet somehow these permutations fail to coalesce,
while searing hatreds and warring sects
revivify premodern norms.

The Look of Silence

The old woman tending to the shadow of a man,
the river running swiftly,
a bridge of sighs,
banana trees, muffled cries for help
in a night that never really died.
Each sequence brings
its own abortive drum call for redemption
and each denial or proud espousal
of what happened on the killing fields
deepens the pain
knowing as we know
that fratricidal divides can never be erased
and that given half a chance
the same characters would play their parts again.

The Look of Silence is the title of a documentary film by Joshua Oppenheimer
on Indonesia, 1965.

Two Images

The image of a tiny boy
washed up on a Turkish shore
flashes around the world
stirring compassion for a people
caught at the extreme
between a despot power-crazed,
and lunatics seeking to wield the prophet's sword.

The image of a little boy
arms aloft as uniformed fanatics of another era
root out the last survivors of the Warsaw Ghetto
flashes through your mind.
And you bow your head in mourning
for what our species can become.

Truth and Consequences

The moment we are named,
we join an extended tribe;
the moment our sex is determined in the womb
(leaving the transgendered to one side),
we are defined;
the moment we are inculcated into a faith,
we leave all others behind.
And then to our surprise,
we find a world divided along predictable battle lines.

Atavisms

Everywhere you look, they're sprouting,
Shiites, Sunnis
rekindling the prophet's avenging spirit,
the Orthodox in countries which had abjured religion,
rediscovering connections
which their autocratic rulers nourish,
retro-Catholics in Poland
preaching intolerance for their opponents,
Hindutva fanatics dreaming of a purified homeland,
Jewish zealots of a reconsecrated Temple Mount,
Buddhist incendiaries in Myanmar,
evangelicals in the New World,
a veritable smorgasbord of beliefs
which a scientific age
had all too hastily dismissed.

The Niqab

The Canadian multiculturalist brigade
is in full flight
to defend the Niqab
as a badge of human rights.
Perhaps it is so
in Yemen's mountain villages or deepest Baluchistan,
but must we honour
every medieval rite
and greet as brethren and sisters
those who frankly shun
the open windows
of our northern home?

The Age of Justin

We turn to history
for storied tales
that linger on,
as the millennials sipping their lattes
embark on the perennial search
for what is young and still untainted.
We are lemmings in our movements
and elections like Geiger counters
measure the subterranean tremors
that tip generations now in one direction, now another,
breathlessly convinced Aquarius will come again
and Camelot soon greet its anointed hour.

Paris XIe

Some years ago
you came to the Canal,
meandering through the market on Richard Lenoir,
sampling pastry from a bakery on the rue Oberkampf,
bathing in the vibrancy
of a newly discovered corner
of the Parisian treasure trove.
Little did you know that twice this year
hammer blows would bring
this tiny haven to *bo-bo* domesticity
to the front-place world stage,
as crusading Islamists wreaked their vengeance
on aliens to their twisted faith.
And so one mourns the slain,
the grievously injured,
the haphazard passersby and city dwellers,
the offspring of modernity
caught up in maelstroms from a darker age.

Lucky Countries

We who live where elections are held
with clock-like predictability,
where you can sleep at night,
make future plans,
never lack for food or drink,
nor doubt that the basic right to speak your mind
will be impinged
can scarcely understand
what the remainder of humanity
experiences in its gut.
For them there is no certainty
the middle ground will hold
that rulers will neither dig in their heels
nor rig the rules,
as a praetorian guard grinds down
those who labour with their bare hands
or dare to step out of line.
Yet the demiurge we dread
also dwells within our gates
in vengeful, polarizing times.

Modernism

Modernism came at a stroke
amidst the carnage and the cold
that swept muddy battlefields,
leaving the old order fractured in its wake.
Scales fell from a generation's eyes,
becoming an atonal twelve,
bodies on canvases disengaged,
squares, cubes and asymmetric blobs
displacing classic harmony for good.
We were growing up,
or so it seemed,
learning to live with bold designs
that swelled until they reached the sky,
movement at a speed
foretelling the eclipse of linear time.
Perhaps the economic data point to sunnier days,
but deep down we sense
the breakdown which the modernists sketched
has become the lethal norm.

The Barbarians

"What are we waiting for, assembled in the public square?
The barbarians are to arrive today."
— Constantine Cavafy, "Expecting the Barbarians"

Are the barbarians really coming,
as Spanish scribes like Pérez-Reverte lament,
or as Cavafy once projected
onto the denizens of Rome's far-off frontiers?
Have we lost our faith
in liberal democracy's underlying ethos,
which for all its imperfections,
mark it off from its despotic, persecuting rivals?
Perhaps we offer the barbarians
a loftier place than they deserve,
perhaps we secretly are becoming
the barbarians whom we dread.

Far from the Imperial Court

Serrated mountains and deep gorges
inspired the Tang poets
seeking a retreat
from a strife-ridden world,
draping themselves in solitude
amidst lush vegetation and bamboo forests
far from the imperial court,
its Great Hall,
and censorious eyes.

Prussia

Prussia lives no more and yet
the vanished kingdom leaves its trace
on sandy shoals and shattered forts
that demarcate the frontiers of the east.
It lives on in martial arts,
in a *realpolitik* that can do no wrong,
in state structures disciplined and strong,
in porcelain of shades so blue,
it leads both sea and sky to cringe.
Was it the monster some believe,
precursor to the gates of hell,
or a land with its own imperfect charm,
where philosophers roamed the aerial sphere,
and the sciences and arts took root,
spreading their wings to other lands?
Prussia lives no more and yet
we speak of her with bated breath.

Inspired by Norman Davies' book *Vanished Kingdoms.*

The Lawgivers

"You write iron laws, Hammurabi, Lycurgus, Solon."
— Anna Akhmatova, "Poem without a Hero"

Multitudes have dwelt under iron laws
through successive ages
or under the hardened yoke
of impermeable religious codes.
To aspire to be free
is to be uncertain,
but to submit
is to shuck off the burden
to some higher power.
The lawgivers of old
knew how to fashion clay with fire.

Vergina

You came to visit these royal tombs,
most probably those of Philip II of Macedon
and his consort,
and the wrought-gold jewellery and silver vessels
are truly regal,
as are the size and scale of the portico
and columns where they lie buried.
Yet something rankles
in this glorification of Macedon,
of Philip and of Alexander
and of the Hellenistic age to follow.
No mention of the king's arch-foe, Demosthenes,
who had rightly seen in him the undoing of the polis.
Instead, it is the force of arms,
the lust for power,
the privileges and rites which follow
that are given the celebratory status
befitting tyrants.

Vergina, originally called Aigai, was the first capital of the ancient
kingdom of Macedonia and the site of the Royal Tombs.

The Authoritarian Impulse

Whitman, in his generous New World fashion,
dreamed of democratic man
and of America offering fresh vistas
for despotic Europe and Asia with their servile throngs.
Dostoyevsky, resurfacing
from his Siberian prison underground,
framed the Grand Inquisitor
with his magic, mystery, and authority
lifting the burden of existential freedom
from humanity's hapless spines.
Who was right and who was wrong
remains in hot dispute,
but as a new century unfolds
the caimans and the crocodiles
are growing bolder.

Brexit

The votes are cast
and the European project
laboriously stitched together over many knittings
begins to badly fray.
Can we really fathom the deep divisions
between the cosmopolitan set of Hampstead Heath
and the North's shattered industrial towns,
between provincials and sophisticates,
school dropouts and matriculates,
a future larger than a county's shires,
a past which cries "Enough!" and "No more!"?
Between the young and super-keen,
Erasmian and European,
and their elders whose borders end at Dover
a chasm beckons.

The Master

"Death is a master from Germany,"
wrote Paul Celan with his staccato lines
and abrogated syllables
in the aftermath of Mitteleuropa's crimes.
And where does death come from today,
as Dhaka's cafés and Ataturk airport's waiting rooms
vie with Nice's Promenade, Aleppo's ruins,
and Juba's killing fields
for space on the front page,
with survivors pouring black libations
over marked and unmarked graves?

History

"History has always been an
immense slaughter house."
— G.W.F. Hegel

One wishes he were wrong,
but flashing lights that mark targets on the ground
and charred bodies
amidst Aleppo's skeletal ruins
remind us
— cocooned in the comfort of our living rooms —
that it is often so,
and though we lucky ones escape,
the luckless ones
await the executioner's appointed hour.

War and Peace

Who was ultimately right,
Kant or Hegel,
the dreamer of peace among the nations,
bound by proper treaties and conventions,
or the heir to Heraclitus,
who saw in war the means to renew civic valour?
The pacifist in us leans invariably to Kant,
struck by the carnage
we see around us.
But the testosterone-driven sort
hanker after that moment of redemption
for ethnic groups, territory, or religion,
and for the camaraderie arising
from the clash of arms.

On a Passage in Kant

"The starry heavens above me and
the moral law within me."
— Immanuel Kant

The stars with their pointillist luminescence
dot the night sky
underlining our glaring insignificance
in the cosmic scheme.
But what about the moral law within
which Kant extolled,
how has it fared in the two centuries
since he walked Königsberg's cobblestones?
Contemplating the Anthropocene,
with the deep inequities that continue to creep in,
and our sapping the finite resources of the earth,
one somehow wishes the stars above
would help us wipe our muddied escutcheon clean.

After Marx

"To hunt in the morning, fish in the afternoon,
critique in the evening after dinner."
— Karl Marx

Perhaps Marx was onto something after all
— now that communism's Big Bang has imploded —
that there is indeed a world beyond alienation,
where the biological clock determines our movements
and you pick and choose how the hours will unfold.
It helps to be plonked down
in a beautiful cove,
on a body of water
that has seen its share of legends,
and have summer's cornucopia close at hand.
It also helps to be free of any obligations,
able to swim or snorkel,
scribble poetry,
prepare your lunchtime meal,
as the spirit moves you.
For a brief season you too can cast aside
the all-too-familiar spectre of estrangement.

Making America Great Again

Once again the pollsters,
those diviners of auspices and entrails,
have been proven wrong,
and the wave of nativist disenchantment
with the Beltway, the urbane elites,
the icons of Wall Street
rolls from the Deep South to the Rust Belt
and across the Plains,
upsetting the political applecart
and giving a new magus carte blanche
to tear up trade deals,
devastate the global climate,
keep foreign riff-raff
from infiltrating liberty's shores.
Where all this will end
only historians of the future will determine,
but for the moment irresistible forces bubble up
from subterranean layers
and *ressentiment* becomes the flavour of the era.

The Demos

The demos can be so fickle,
excoriating the first honest politician
they've ever seen
— an Alfonsin in Argentina,
a Gorbachev in the ex-USSR —
because economically times were tough,
or a rotten old regime had finally bitten the dust,
embracing the most loathsome and corrupt
— a Berlusconi or a Trump —
trafficking notoriety and pilfered wealth
for naked power.
It makes one almost despair
of the larger creed we westerners so earnestly profess,
forgetting how democracy among the ancients
had its share of assemblies easily swayed
by demagogues and knaves
for every Pericles or Demosthenes that came along.

Canada at 150

"We don't need any Kaiser"
— Heinrich Heine "A Winter's Tale"

What courage, back in 1843,
for the bard to give voice
to what was a faint stirring
somewhere in the forest depths
of a Germany still awaiting
a springtime of the people.
And we,
in this Dominion of the North,
who have been sleeping for a full 150 years,
putting up with regal flummery,
with all the trappings of Old World monarchy,
have yet to break with a mentality
that harks back to our colonial bonds.

Sesquicentenary

You would have been more acerbic
in your salad years,
convinced that our somnolent Dominion of the North
had missed a historical beat or two,
spurning revolutions,
holding on for dear life to the apron strings
of two empires in rapid succession,
our leaders always reaching for the middle,
few clear goals to excite the imagination.

Now that you're a senior
and Canada's even more so,
your former disdain has given way
to a spirit of reconciliation.
It isn't easy managing a country
with awkward platelets that see themselves
as distinct nations, with far-flung regions
and a macédoine of peoples
which elsewhere might incite internecine hatreds.

We have fended off the worst traits
of the giant to the south,
while living reasonably amicably beside it.
Our social compass resembles that of Europe
and our vision of the world order
combines a Boy Scout's earnestness for alliances
with a penchant for UN-sanctioned conventions.

We have had our share of failings:
the excessive influence of corporations,
foreign and domestic,
politicians who line their pockets,
policies that haven't really helped
to integrate First Nations,
closed doors to refugees in the '30s
wartime deportation of innocent civilians.

But in the larger scheme of things
we haven't screwed up too badly,
neither plumbing the depths of failed or fragile states
nor suffering from despotic rulers,
though we've sometimes come quite close
with autocratic premiers and nepotistic tribal chiefs.

Still, you don't feel out of place
lifting a glass to Canada's sesquicentenary,
much as you might prefer more pizzazz and drama
in a country which has learned to live in peace.

– IV –

MEDITATIONS AND
REFLECTIONS

Iolkos

"And Iolkos, which had grown rich, was
destroyed by revolts and tyrannical government."
— Strabo

In a history of Magnesía
Strabo's curt phrase
is all that has come down to us
of the fate of dynasties
that followed on the *Argo*,
while tales of usurping Pelias,
one-sandalled Jason and his avenging wife,
echo and resound.
This town once rich and prosperous,
vanished without trace
in the Dark Ages that felled Mycenae's palaces.
Petty feuds among rival claimants to the throne,
struggles between landowners and kings,
a hint of popular revolt —
who can piece from clay fragments
and lava bits around the mound
a full account of what transpired?
Of kingly Iolkos and its fate
the air, the rocks,
and Pagasetic waters
remain the sole custodians.

_____

Iolkos was an ancient city (now the contemporary city of Volos) located
on a gulf of the Aegean known as the Pagasitikos and was, according to
legend, the place from which Jason and the *Argo* sailed.

Theomachy

To have dared to question
what fear of the unknown, the unspoken had instilled,
to have been sceptics when others built their altars,
burnt their offerings,
sought oracles and gateways to the divine
was to frame the universe
out of material building blocks.
Few were the rewards for daring to stand out,
many the dangers in casting doubt
where others wrapped themselves
in the certainties of unbridled faith,
comforted by avatars
with magical powers over life and death.
They were few, all too few in ancient times,
yet their probing thoughts were not in vain,
and we who follow in their path today
can belatedly claim them as our own.

"Theomachy" means opposition to God or the gods or the divine will.
The poem was inspired by my reading of Tim Whitmarsh's *Battling
the Gods: Atheism in the Ancient World.*

Orpheus

It's no easy gambit
to follow in his footsteps,
knowing that busking has low status
in a high-tech age,
that the obstacles to entering Hades
are no less fearsome than before,
that the venture will end badly,
even if one could pry one's loved one
onto the pathway out of the underworld
for the briefest of moments.
Still, like jilted lovers,
grieving ones have been known
to persist against all logic
attempting to recover
what has been lost forever,
seeking to storm
the gates of hell or heaven,
with tears, songs, imprecations,
and suicidal gestures
— all for nothing.

The Beach

Giordano Bruno was inspired
on a beach at Noli
to project planetary systems
equivalent to ours upon the distant stars
and for this intuition and others like it
forfeited his life to the Inquisition.
A fate to ponder
as summers on a Mediterranean beach
stoke pleasures of the moment.

Rousseau

Jean-Jacques still haunts us,
though his sensibility was overwrought,
his educational dicta too utopian to be taught,
his social contract too ingenious for our lot.
Perhaps it is his personality, tortured, manic, twisted,
his contradictions, an imperfect reflection of our own,
his iconoclastic fury when reason wove its constricting arc,
his communion with a nature swirling all around.
His was a voice that stood out from the others,
a pen that seemed to take a Sybil as its guide,
a springboard to the splintered modern project
where fortune's outcasts
jostle with the rich and powerful
for a mere moment in the sun.

Salon World

Reading about Madame Helvétius
and her salon at Auteuil,
her dalliance with Franklin —
"all those days for only one night" —
and lofty conversations with Turgot, Cabanis, Condorcet
and other apostles of the Enlightenment,
you almost commit the folly Montaigne had warned against
of wishing you had lived several centuries ago,
forgetting in the process the poorhouses,
the abandoned children, the incurables wallowing in their filth,
even as the literary and scientific comets of their age
glittered up above.

Condorcet

To retain his composure
even when proscribed
was feat enough.
To sketch out a future
for humankind
that builds on genuine empathy
for the underdog
while hiding from the Terror
was nobler still.
To not forsake his faith
in reason, science
and the revolution's enduring principles
when fanaticism was closing in
gives even the most sceptical
cause to catch their breath.

Nicolas de Condorcet is the author of the *Esquisse d'un tableau historique des progrès de l'esprit humain,* 1794. He perished at the tail end of the Reign of Terror.

In Hölderlin's Footsteps

"Seeliges Griechenland! du Haus der Himmlischen alle."
— Friedrich Hölderlin, "Brod und Wein"

Can it really be so,
he who never set foot
in the celestial ones' home,
but dreamt of it with an exile's fervour?

Can myths ever come true —
surging waves against clapping rocks,
islands scattered like brittle gems
or the morning dew
under an overwrought sun,
all this in a Greece
which remains enshrined in a past,
where legends were freshly forged
and the Olympians could share a repast or two
with mere mortals?

Hölderlin flew too high
and like Icarus
came crashing down to earth,
but his passionate verse resounds
in a land once beloved of the gods.

Johan Huizinga's Homo Ludens

O Dutch sage, who deciphered the principle of play
even as madmen sat atop your world
and the mask of tragedy would soon dispel
the ritual verse or bantering lines
that heralded our civilized flights of fancy.
The riddle remains unresolved,
how cruelty and love,
darkness and light,
jests of love and jousts of war
so easily coincide
within the hard-wired carapace
of our species,
how little we have advanced,
for all our playfulness,
from barbarous uses of the human mind.

The Hampels

In harrowing times
a solitary worker and his wife
decide to put their wherewithal
into penning cards
that speak their resistance to a regime
sending millions of its own
(and tens of other millions)
to their demise.
They drop these off on window sills in office buildings
until one day the guillotine comes down
and they face as stoically as they can
the Gestapo's Argus eyes.
Such is the fate of those who die alone,
yet leave a fleeting mark,
a quickened beating of the heart
in those who will live hereafter.

Inspired by my reading of Hans Fallada's *Every Man Dies Alone* — about
Elise and Otto Hampel.

A Poet's Shadow

His journey through the Greek landscape
and the archaeology of ruined antiquity
is quaintly Mitteleuropean.
So too a soft spot for Piero della Francesca,
Montaigne's Italian musings,
or Latin fragments culled
from his *gymnasium* years.
Where he comes into his own
is in his evocation of the defenceless Templars,
the travesties of the Nazi doctors,
the poet's need to plant his standard
beyond a field of mindless prattle.
He meditated deeply,
combing the classics,
turning irony into a lethal weapon
in an era when evil triumphed copiously
over its innumerable victims.
A legacy not to be ignored.

Inspired by my reading of Zbigniew Herbert's *The Collected Prose, 1948–1998*
as well as by his poems.

L'Écriture ou la Vie

Once more dawn's light,
this time with a halting fear —
we are at Buchenwald's gate.
Through what particular grace
did some remain alive,
how from our species' deepest reservoirs
did others summon up lines
to keep their sanity afloat?
Like shooting stars
the camp survivors one by one
slip off the noose of life.
Will we ever be quite done
with this nightmare's telling?

Inspired by reading Jorge Semprún, a Spanish writer and politician who,
having survived Buchenwald, lived in France most of his life and wrote
primarily in French.

The Pilgrim

How difficult to betray
principles that marked your youth,
to inhabit a state which has vanished
and join one to which you can never belong.
How strange the loyalties
to promises that were never kept,
to symbols that were only fleetingly true,
to a code that outsiders would never understand
for they cannot experience
what was lived from inside.
So you take your pilgrim's staff
to the far shore of another continent,
seeking in the soil where émigrés flocked,
in sunsets, ocean vistas and endless table talk
clues to the strange predicament
that is not only yours
but that of others who yearn
for that impossible fusion between ideals
and compromises that always leave us short.

Christa Wolf, one of the leading writers of the former G.D.R. (East
Germany), spent the year after the fall of the Berlin Wall at a cultural
institute in Los Angeles, where she penned the book *City of Angels* that
inspired this poem.

On Some Lines in Seferis

"The middle-aged feel growing wider
the gap between the body
that drags behind them like a wounded camel
and the soul with its courage inexhaustible, as they say."
— George Seferis, "Stratis the Sailor by the Dead Sea"

Never until now had you felt the gap
quite as the poet described it.
Earlier you could slough off, behind a veil of work,
or seamless talk,
the hour of reckoning.
Ignoring the *longue durée,*
you could make much of political events
or shifting intellectual habits.
But alone in this room,
overlooking a Pelion
that never ceases to work its magic,
you stumble upon this passage by Seferis.
And suddenly your feet drag,
and you feel the decades
harrowing your bones and marrow.

The Alexandria Quartet

The characters bind and unwind,
storms rage from the sea,
elegant cafés line the Cornice
as the human comedy,
the dogs of war on the loose,
unfolds like a Japanese fan,
while the Poet looks on
with the eyes of an owl
and the weight of 2000 years.
"Farewell Alexandria,"
you are tempted to say,
though you have never really been there,
for this city of pleasure
is a wisp of conceit,
a phantom that taunts,
a Pharos that beckons
on the cusp of the desert sands.

A Northern Lyre

Another Orpheus
to join the rhymesters
along the bedevilled shore,
the mood is Slavic,
winter frost to glaze the windows,
plastered ceiling, dusty chandelier.
Yet Narcissus in the mirror
flashes half a smile,
and the body, the sinful body
is on fire down below.

Inspired by Vladislav Khodasevich's *Selected Poems*.

Sentimental Education

"He thought himself handsome, and
lingered for a minute to gaze at his image."
— Frédéric Moreau in *L'Éducation sentimentale*

His glance could melt the very glass into which he gazed,
for had the world ever witnessed beauty so wondrous
it moved the very elements to tears?
More than himself he loved
the deep brooding of the eyes,
hair so perfect in its patterning,
nose and lips bespeaking the heroic pose
of chiselled art.
And so he craved what was beyond attainment,
a freezing of the moment,
spared forever the decrepitude of age.

On Re-reading Neruda's
"The Heights of Macchu Picchu"

You have read and re-read these stanzas
soaring with condors into thin air
haunted by death's shadow,
rubbing stones hewn by tremulous hands,
surveying ruins reposing on terraced earth,
like stalks of corn
shrouded by mist and overgrown foliage.
Only a maestro could dare what he attempted,
towers of language
cascading like water through conduits
to temples and villas,
reaching out to the humble
who toiled so their lords could flourish
in a stillness harder than quartz.

Fidelity

The hypocrite in us searches for words,
to forge carnal bonds to appease our lust.
Those who like Odysseus have wandered far and wide,
have found a Calypso in every port
to stoke an exile's fire,
while Penelope languishes with her fleece.
Some wines one sips are ruby deep,
others the rose of strawberries,
still others a white that refreshes the heart
and keeps the body trim.
So the songs men sing
are but excuses summoned up
to wash away the evidence.
The lines remain faithful,
even when the flesh cannot.

Bitter Oranges

So much will remain unsaid and undone,
as blazing sun turns days
into tortured intervals
and windless nights prey heavily on sleep.
A gentle word or two might have made a difference
a simple touch or caressing of the hair,
but he was too proud in his silly masculine way
and she was too hurt,
and by then they were miles apart
and bitter oranges were in season.

In the Literary Café

Philosophers can scarce be trusted
in legislating for a democratic state.
Think of Plato acting as adviser to Syracuse's tyrants
and dreaming of a perfectly regimented republic,
or Heidegger toadying to the Nazis
and their murderous Volk-ish creed.

But poets, despite Shelley's optimistic dictum,
can prove scarcely any better.
Borges, no mean scribbler,
had a soft spot for the Argentinian and Chilean juntas,
Pound collaborated with the fascists,
as for the Great Helmsman Mao,
who deemed himself a poet after all,
the tens of millions who succumbed
in the Great Leap Forward
and the millions in the Cultural Revolution
were not mere tropes.

A bit of modesty, waiter,
along with the drinks,
when you next serve rounds
in the literary café.

Lost Lines

Cryptic words like ones the Pythia might have spoken,
at Delphi in Apollo's temple
or the blighted songs of nightingales in laurel trees,
or lost lines of the tragedians one can never retrieve.

The Obscure Hours

Poets must prefer the obscure hours,
3 to 6 AM before the sun has risen
and the sky begins to take on colour,
while others are asleep
and will not sense the strange configurations
going through their minds,
when the silence carves deep imprints
where most are hesitant to venture,
for once daylight has broken
so has the spell,
and a different voice takes over
purpose-driven, *Zweckrational.*

Zweckrational: instrumentally rational.

Land's End

An orange moon was in the sky,
so close at hand,
it seemed to graze the condo towers
and greet joggers along the beach
like a hostess offering margaritas and dips
to start the evening off.
It was a mirage, of course,
for soon enough it would take its austere place
in a firmament of bartered West Coast hopes.

The Burden of the Past

The immensity of the poetic corpus can overwhelm,
Chinese classics, Persian mystics,
Lorca's *duende*,
the silver verse of the Russian avant-garde,
a whirl of mimetic sound and dervish energy.

It leaves some yearning for more familiar ground,
the playful turning of words inside out or upside down
that goes viral in a digital age.

Perhaps by immersing themselves in the here and now,
they can shuck off the pain of communing with the past,
ignoring the insidious workings of time,
believing they can storm literary citadels
with a few hyped-up lines.

Ballad of Farewell

In parting we find
the city of our dreams dissolving
into an impossibility of feeling
where no night or morning will ever be the same.
We promise to preserve its namesakes
in some perfect mind frame
but we know these are idle words
that sleet and snow will wash away,
leaving a fado melody to pluck the heart strings.

Inspired by Fernando Machado Soares' "Balada da Despedida," sung every
spring by the graduating class in law at the University of Coimbra, Portugal's
oldest university.

The City

"You said I will go to another land . . . to another sea.
Always you will arrive in this city. Do not hope for any other."
— Constantine Cavafy, "The City"

When the poet evoked his Alexandria,
could he have guessed
he spoke a quasi-universal truth?
Our wanderlust may take us
to distant places
as our restless hearts seek solace
in exotic cultures, landscapes, symbiotic interfacing.
Yet we are drawn back
as in a whirlpool that enlaces
what we cannot abandon,
to the fixed markers of childhood and adolescence,
to familiar patterns of societal interaction,
to river or sea with its changing moods and currents,
to mountains that frame a tiny corner piece of heaven,
to where — for better or for worse —
our dreams are realized and perish.

– V –

THANATOS'S
SHADOW

The Triumph of Death

This is the third time
— your third visit to the Prado —
that you have been drawn to this painting,
haunted by the battle of the dead with the living,
with its details of kings, noble women
and simple peasant wretches
succumbing to Thanatos's swollen legions.
This time there is a poignancy to your meeting,
Bruegel's own death short of forty — or was it forty-five? —
seemingly foretold in his overcrowded canvas,
a warning to the visitor to be *en garde.*

In the Archaeological Museum

They reach across an invisible divide,
here the spouse, the daughter of the house,
an elder snatched away,
a youth, a child.
We see their silhouettes sketched in stone,
the silence of the tomb
reflected in the tender gaze
and impossible touching of the hands
as the living world one last time
embraces the world of the dead.
How beautiful, yet how estranged,
the museum rooms echoing to the sounds
of school children herded through,
and tourists snapping pictures
they know instinctively will not endure.

Moonlit Paths

"The moonlit paths of the departed."
— Georg Trakl

You know they are long gone
but somehow when they filter
through your dreams
or a smell, a sound
triggers reminiscence
you are ready to dissolve
into a cloud of powder-puff nostalgia
past all false moorings and deserted islands
where you once alighted,
nestling in a tiny alcove
awaiting daylight's stirring.

The Ferryman

To dwell on your own demise
is to engage in an age-old trope.
It is to sweep Eros to one side,
allowing Thanatos to occupy centre stage,
dancing the macabre dance
that parodies the grave.
Years of preparation and artistic emulation
carry little suasion
when the ferryman asks for his fare.
"It's still only an obol," he proclaims,
"a veritable bargain when you factor in inflation."
He's right, of course,
but only the foolhardy
are eager to embark.

On Reading Machado

Machado wrote with broken heart
for the one he buried,
coupled with inspired vision
of the Iberian landscape,
flowering brambles, acacias,
olive trees hugging the hilltops,
sensitive to echoes of the generation of 1898,
Castilian pride reduced to shambles.

You have no empire to lament
and West Coast nature is luxuriant
with its kaleidoscope of foliage and flora.
But the stress your loved one carries,
like a primordial curse the fates have spun,
haunts your spirit.

Antonio Machado, a Spanish poet who lived from 1875–1939, lost his wife
after three short years of marriage. Like other Spanish writers, he was much
affected by Spain's defeat in the Spanish-American War of 1898.

Stabat Mater

We aspire to a sphere,
where voices no longer hug the ground
but merge with heavenly sounds
to lift us from the finitude where we expire.
And though we cannot escape our fate
and know it in our hearts,
we seek solace of a sort
in what has driven others
to sacred music as a consolatory art.

Night Poem

A heavy cloud shrouds this house,
for you can sense the hollow in her eyes,
the panic which fresh assaults against her body set off,
the certainty that her demise
comes closer with each lengthening day.
So little joy in what you write
in the faltering twilight where she struggles on.

Night Vigil

A 2 AM vigil turns into 4,
her osteopenia spreading,
hips barely functioning
as each excruciating step
makes her regret the step ahead.
Alpha and omega have come undone,
rapid beating of her pulse is like a clock
relentlessly dragging her along,
as the throbbing in her head won't stop.

For Mahie

When you have gone
and your arm, your one good arm,
will no longer brush my face
what will keep your memory alive?
Pictures from your youth,
Paris, May '68,
a garret room just off the rue St. Jacques?
Vancouver beckoning,
Kits where we first set roots,
Point Grey where we nurtured one another
for over forty years?
Thessaly on countless summer visits,
night sky over Pelion,
chestnut trees, centaur trails?
These will remain as talismans
beyond your tormented final years.

Decline

As days turn into weeks,
you sense the impasse she has reached,
the near impossibility of standing
on her own two feet,
or regaining autonomy
over her rudimentary needs.
Layer by layer,
dignity is stripped away,
as the monotony of time
drains the will to overcome.

You Looked Pretty

You looked pretty in your chair,
your eyes alert and rested,
as though injuries serially inflicted
had been deftly swept aside.
You looked pretty in the light
of our four decades together,
faithful companion to sometimes troubled moments,
a beacon through the fog and strife.
You looked pretty despite the tubes
that filtered blood and heartache too,
resisting as best you could
Atropos's sinister hand.

Atropos, the oldest of the three Fates, known as the "Inevitable," cut the thread of life with her shears.

Last Days

Soon this will not be her home
and the tiny things of everyday,
toast and jam, shared cups of tea,
the rituals of shampooing her hair
or preparing her sandwich for the dialysis ordeal
will disappear.
No one with whom to share
a thought or two at night,
no quarrelling over petty things
or holding fast to those that count.
Daphnes wilt and desperate thoughts bloom.

Hemodialysis Ward

One by one they peel away,
the stout one with his hearty countenance
and shiny eyes,
the thin one with her flimsy garb
and tinsel voice,
the ones who've lost a leg or two,
the one whose heart could not sustain the toll,
the one whose blood could not be staunched,
the one who could not swallow food —
the list grows longer by the day,
you shudder knowing who is next in line.

Hospital Vigil

Each visit brings its own impossibilities,
breathing difficulties, fluid overload,
waning appetite, digestive challenges,
and with these the death-rattle melancholy
of her spirit.
How much longer can she hold out
against the natural order,
what comforting words or gestures
can rouse her from her reclining bed
to rejoin the chorus of the hopeful?

Genealogy

A son comes to visit,
embraces, get-well cards from the grandkids,
words of encouragement
in a struggle with little prospect of emendation.
He will leave tonight,
and the fourth week of her Calvary will begin,
restless nights, constricted hospital space,
rounds of physio and dialysis stretching to the horizon.
In the genealogy our son will compose,
hers will be an honoured name
alongside those who have already perished.

Intermezzo

Sail on, sail on,
though your heart is broken,
the horizon beset with raging maelstroms,
leaving no haven and no calm.
Try to find a rudder, if you can,
a balm to keep the grief at bay,
for what has now befallen her
can never be undone.

I Have Become My Country

The chronometer counts down
on a debt that will never be repaid
on a currency union that won't cohere
on a land whose inhabitants
treat public finance and taxation
as something from an alien sphere.

So too her chronometer counts down,
chronic illnesses that cannot be effaced,
energy levels in permanent decline,
a physiology in helpless disrepair,
her autonomy subject to forces
beyond her power.

"I have become my country," she declares,
as Greece careens from crisis into crisis.

Purdy Pavilion, UBC

Sallow faces, sunken sockets,
wheelchairs clogging hallways,
time that sets its hands in backward motion,
hoists to lift the infirm,
commodes to clean them,
circle games and regulated feedings,
the extreme boundaries of survival.

Euridyce

*"She was deep within herself
and did not see the man in front
or the path ascending steeply into life."*
— Rilke, "Orpheus. Euridyce. Hermes"

Rilke's evocation haunts you,
the dark pond, the meandering path,
the god of messages
lightly rubbing against the dead mortal's shroud.
Orpheus walks ahead,
his lyre packed away,
intent to capture the sound of footsteps behind —
in vain.
But Eurydice pivots the poem,
oblivious to all the goings-on,
not even certain who this shade
— she has forgotten flesh and blood —
who has turned to look at her might be.
"Who," she wonders
as Hermes takes her along the pathway down.
"Who," a word that lingers
as your own companion retreats
from worldly concerns
into her shadow realm.

The Swallow

The swallow that heralds the spring
has flown away,
only a vacant nest remains
with a few solitary twigs strewn on the ground
as the sun climbs high
greeting the archipelago
that frames her native land.
She lies in crumpled hospital sheets
which constitute her last retreat,
and who knows what words unformed
are stillborn in a brain
that has endured a second fatal blow
even as each laboured breath
drains what dwindling force remains?
All too soon
she'll join those whom she first knew
and those who perish
in the conflicts and calamities
of our age.
Yet your heart recalls the swallow
of those halcyon days,
the one that now with tattered wings
will never fly away.

On Solitude

"When the time comes to lose them."
— Michel de Montaigne

Enjoy the fruits of the earth,
the pleasures of youth,
travel's enchantment,
the conviviality of your favourite companions.
Experience love in close quarters,
and learn to share with your mate
the wonders of growing older
and taking counsel from each other.
But prepare for what must follow,
as body parts go rigid,
skin and flesh prove brittle,
and the one who was the pillar of your heart
departs before you.

Ave atque vale

Catullus set off on a lonely journey
to the near ends of his known world
to mourn his brother.
And you have come
to the tiny piece of earth
she venerated above all others
to mourn her passing.

Ave atque vale: Hail and farewell.

The Portrait

for Vassia Karambelias

The portrait on the wall
painted fifty years ago
in her Paris student years
by a devoted friend
stares down on you.
And though sunshine bathes the hallway
of her parental home
as the early morning clouds retreat,
a plangent mood pervades
the shuttered sitting room.

Gratitude and Grieving

Gratitude and grieving rarely coalesce
but in returning here
you find them curiously conjoined.
This house, refurbished,
brings back innumerable memories
of when the kids were young,
when she and I and they
could spend the summer months
beneath Pelion's canopy.

Arriving here alone,
conscious that the pebbles on the beach
and the rolling waves
are forever beyond her reach,
triggers a second round of mourning,
as though tragedy dwelt
in this epicentre of stark beauty.
Yet tragedy is commingled
with grateful recognition
of the waters and rocky spires
that inspired the ancients and the muses.

Agios Tachiarchis

You push the boundaries of despair
hoping that faces from the past
will spring miraculously
from behind the stone retainer walls
and fountain in the square
where children played
and villagers danced summer nights away.

But the months which saw her to the grave
become like bridesmaids
whose raiments slowly fade
into the nether sphere
as the voice you desperately seek
no longer whispers in your ear.

Agios Tachiarchis is a part of the village of Tsagarada on Mount Pelion
where, as a family, we spent many summers.

The Enchanted Cove

Tourists stop to linger
at the magic of the spot,
the cove with its surrounding cliffs,
the thickness of the old stone walls
that serve as bulwarks for the house,
wondering when it may have been built,
and when fixed up.
They are right,
something of the fantastic
hovers over both cove and house,
transfixing those who come this way.
But with her passing
something other than enchantment
lingers in your heart.

Darkness

Darkness rushes to engulf you
much like a rising sea
and though baroque music in the background
ought to calm you,
it cannot.
Absence preys more heavily than presence,
nighttime than day,
and in these early hours
the lost one you strive to talk to
seems just beyond your reach.
A word, a gesture,
might seem to bring her closer
but what you hear instead
is an echo in your head.
"Stay," you want to say
with all the passion you can summon,
"do not leave me now,"
yet the darkness has no answer
to a grieving with no cure.

On Revisiting a Cavafy Poem

"And say farewell to the Alexandria you are losing."
— Constantine Cavafy, "The Gods Desert Antony"

What was it you so feared to lose
on leaving Damouchari many years ago
with Takis, himself now dead,
reciting the final verse from Cavafy's poem
as you all headed up from the cove?
Was it the possibility of transposing into words
the murmuring waves, the light evening breeze,
the sun preparing to fade
on the opposite side of the cliffs?
Was it regarding any certainty
as to when you might all return,
with the stone walls and parapet
bearing silent witness to your earlier passage?
Was it a premonition
of the acrid bitterness entailed
in losing the one you loved above all others?

ABOUT THE AUTHOR

Philip Resnick began writing poetry in Montreal, stopping for a time when he embarked on an academic career at the University of British Columbia. His marriage to Andromache (Mahie), who was Greek, resulted in numerous stays in Thessaly, in the city of Volos, and in a village on adjacent Mount Pelion. These stays rekindled his poetic inspiration and resulted in the publication of a number of collections in the late 1970s and 1980s. Philip has continued to write ever since and has published numerous poems in magazines and journals, as well as a 2015 collection entitled *Footsteps of the Past*. As a political scientist at the University of British Columbia for over forty years until his retirement in 2013, Philip has published widely on political topics. He makes his home in Vancouver, British Columbia.

MARQUIS

Québec, Canada